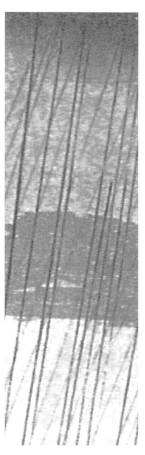

TEN THOUSAND VIEWS OF RAIN

TEN THOUSAND VIEWS OF RAIN

Terry Watada

THISTLEDOWN PRESS

© Terry Watada, 2001
All rights reserved

No part of this publication may be reproduced or transmitted in any form or by any means, graphic, electronic or mechanical, including photocopying, recording, or any information storage and retrieval system, without permission in writing from the publisher. Requests for photocopying of any part of this book shall be directed in writing to CanCopy, 1 Yonge Street, Suite 1900, Toronto, Ontario, M5C 1E5.

Canadian Cataloguing in Publication Data

Watada, Terry
Ten thousand views of rain
ISBN 1-894345-24-X
I. Title.
PS8595.A79T46 2001   C811'.54   C2001-910253-4
PR9199.3.W3688T46 2001

Cover: Detail from *Ohashi Bridge and Atake in Sudden Shower*, from the series *One Hundred Views of Famous Places in Edo*, Ando Hiroshige
Cover and book design by J. Forrie
Typeset by Thistledown Press Ltd.
Printed and bound in Canada

Thistledown Press Ltd.
633 Main Street
Saskatoon, Saskatchewan
S7H 0J8

Thistledown Press gratefully acknowledges the financial assistance of the Canada Council for the Arts, the Saskatchewan Arts Board, and the Government of Canada through the Book Publishing Industry Development Program for its publishing program.

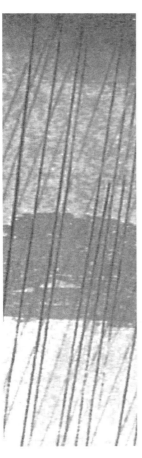

TEN THOUSAND VIEWS OF RAIN

Poems in this collection originally appeared in the following journals:

Canadian Literature, Cranberry Tree Anthology, Dalhousie Review, Intangible, Kalliope: a journal of women's art, Millennium Messages (a publication of the Asian Canadian Writers Workshop), *MoonRabbit Review, Other Voices, Paper Boat, The Toronto Review, Vintage 1999, White Wall Review.*

"Sisters to the Rain" received an honourable mention in the *Other Voices* poetry competition (Fall 2000).

"Counting Koden" received an honourable mention in the Cranberry Tree Anthology poetry competition (Summer 2000).

"City of Fallen Angels" won the 1996 *MoonRabbit Review* poetry competition in Boulder, Colorado.

I would like to thank Tane Akamatsu and Bunji for their patience, love and understanding. A special thank you to Rosemary Stackhouse for her keen insights and inspiration.

Much gratitude to George Payerle and Susan Musgrave for helping me see the poems in a clear light.

— Terry Watada
December, 2000

CONTENTS

THE RAIN CANTOS

Dear Miss Kim	12
Waiting For Rain	14
The Return of the Trades	16
The Taste of Rain	17
The Storm	18
the Eye of the Storm	20
Sisters to the Rain	21
Childhood	25
Ghost on the Water	26
remembering the rain	27
Chasing the Rain	28

U[TA-GO]KORO

Mango Summer	34
The Emperor of Stars	35
and I saw an angel	36
and in my half-sleep/	
I heard *Otōsan* leaving	38
Kiss of a Father	39
A Simple Face	41
Talk Story	42
Childhood	44
Counting *Kōden*	45
Kona Weather	48
Broken Moon	49
Sisters	50

The Swimming Pool	52
Nightclouds	54
Eating Figs with Mrs. Long	55
Lushlife	57
a light rain in New Orleans	62
Beneath the Southern Cross	64
By the Buddha Bar	66
Seattle: *pacific jazz*	68
10,000 Views of Diamond Head	69
Paper Lanterns in August	71
City of Fallen Angels	74
Another Home	79

NIKKEI MONOGATARI: Impressions of the Japanese-Canadian Internment Experience

A View from "The Orchard"	82
The Irony of First Snow	83
Stillness	85
Wild Strawberries and Mushrooms	88
Moon Above the Ruins	89
The Sound of a Train	91
An Empty Field	93
Bury Your Horses	95
A Funeral in the Mountains	98

GLOSSARY	99

for Mrs. Grace Akamatsu and Mrs. Kay Shin

The Rain Cantos

Dear Miss Kim

Our son is
        gentle as a rain-
wash on an april morning
his hair
   delicate, the colour
of light on grass
at dawn

his eyes
   black whirlpools
pulling in
all that can be seen

and he sings to me,
having no words
to say,
a song only
he has learned
before time

and my
       wife
laughs his laugh
in
   celebration

       our son
will dream of you
during
       April showers

as I listen
to your pentatonic blues:

> *the tokyo rain*
> *can never wash away*
> *my Korean stain*

Dear Miss Kim,

That part of you
    that is within him
and not welcome
in Japan

is welcome here.

for the adopted

Waiting for Rain

her curved
back
    rests against
the Adirondack
chair
    as the country
night
   fills with jazz
fire-flies ignite
  in a frenzied
scale
as dizzy's trumpet hits
those notes 5/4 to the bar

her long dead daughter
chatters over the slow
blues of billie holy-day

new york humidity
during that long august
night,
   when
      heroin carried
the weight
  of her child's cries
(empty echoes
in a hospital room and
around
  a building
of no sympathy as
the outside
    sweltered),

pressed against her with
the stickiness of memory

a slight wind mounts

her back uncurls
with the cat-like
approach of rain.

The Return of the Trades
(on new year's eve)

distant roar
of rain   approaches

sweep sweep the old
out of
every corner
      hurry hurry
paper gods
sopping wet in the wind
   the *kami* flutter

that which
    awaits us in
the new year
begins
      with
    rain
and
    the return of the trades

The Taste of Rain

the window faces
the street   no wind
no rain (no
longer)
        comes through
the fine mesh
of storm window
to touch
the skin with its mild
acid

[yet I can taste the rain
in (her presence] is
invisible to the sight)
        familiar to the smell
but acrid to the taste

thighs mould
to shoulders
arms tighten
together in the
f(r)iction of
sweat & emotion

when mist sprays
through the window
        the rain
lingers
        on the tongue

The Storm

air
   molten with
a heavy
golden light
   washes against
city buildings

until the faces
in the street
hide
   in the grey
anticipating rain

        like turner
        lashed to the mast   his
        eyes peeled in horror
        as god approached

wind tousles
   news and paper
window shutters
rattle   within
a   thunder-
       clap

but the storm is dry
without sheen of wetness
deepening of
colour   nor hope of vision

        unlike turner
        who felt the wet slap
        of god's hand
        against his face
        and saw the storm
        as a blur of paint
        on canvas

unlike the self
    the storm-void
spreading
  before me

my eyes
  burning   derided
by vanity
     pulling me in
tearing me apart

the Eye of the Storm

With the
      sudden
gasp of
air
      wind
dark
  and nightmare
        torn
     words spill   images
shatter   her breath
is shocked
she lies as if dead

as pigs snuffle
  at the feet   filipino women
chatter
    an insane language
and the hand
  of god rides
the swirling winds
through
      the windows:

the ragged whispers of a distant hurricane.

Sisters to the Rain

Ayako likes to sit
in the dark, listening
to Bird
      sipping in
liquor needles   pulling in
smoke from all parts
of the room
and feeling close
to the rain
          outside

she would've married

but he was a married man
who promised
he would leave and never did

   like the doctor
within the madness
  of secrets
never revealing himself

and the asian man
who practised love through
suffocation

      a sister to the rain

    the drain of alcohol
        within Sumiko
chastens her
        dulls her
presses
    down
  upon her

her father
draped the *hinomaru*
above her every night

    she slept beneath the imperial
    glory of the pacific the sun
    rose and burst

beneath her closed eyes

    crack of the bamboo
for failure,
    disobedience
disgrace

    a sister to the rain

the bloodshot flush
of anger
reason falling to blindness
   rage races up the throat
     and
vomits
      a
        word
spill
of daggers and toxin

      a sister to the rain

~~~

tears
   in a storm
hold no one
in its cold touch,
its humid cling

yet the 2 sisters
stand in welcome
of the storm   over
the grave
   of their sister
fumi
     whose name
was *Fumiko* (stripped
of beauty, eyes

and contour
    girlhood lost in the *ko*
of her buried name
        expunged
from the gravestone)

faces straight up
    mouths
open
        drinking
in the drizzling
onslaught

with
    sadness about the eyes
a triplet
        of sisters
in crying rain.

Childhood

      the bruise
oozes like a suffocating ink
across the child's face
         the moon
slides to hide its light
as if in shame

and the hands
desperately sink
beneath the rafters
of the chest
to spread the ribs
in an effort to breathe

a father   crushes his heart

the rain pours
steadily steady (in)stead

Ghost on the Water

I saw her
wrapped in morning fog
spotted
      with rain

translucent white
skin
    wrapped
in grief
      her feet tickling
waves   not drowning
 tears in a stream
      down
that shattered, still
fragile face

I saw her
just the other day
      wrapped
in the arms
of a husband who remembered
her
while in the freefall
of doubt
      and betrayal

from the Viaduct

remembering the rain

the house
        is darker than usual
the rain outside
calls
with muted complaints
as tiny fists rapping
        against windows and roof.

the hands of music
ripple
through stereo mouths
with the rain
on the street.

        bill evans plays,
        lofaro under-
          pins
        the jazz of late evening.

the seduction of strangers:
        eyes
meet and then divert
lips
   press and then release
            limbs
embrace and then open.

i remember the rain
the night that poet-
ghosts *in flagrante*
dissolved
into the wet streets.

Chasing the Rain

I was driving
in the Delta region
      the land flat, drying
in the sun   the bottom of the valley
hidden in shadows
     when
I saw on the horizon
a wound
of bad weather
     behind me

I had left a
     blinding
rain
it was as if I were in
the slipstream of light   coming from darkness
       and chasing headlong into darkness

her face formed before me
in greeting

her eyes round
with age & ill-
ness
     the pupils clouded
almost blind
but she smiled   in recognition

   a bank of clouds
      above the unsettled horizon
amassing

              cumulus upon cirrus
moisture within moisture
                the thunderhead
accumulated above
as the dark scar of a downpour
emptied
     below

Listen to the rhythm
of the falling rain

rose cadences
     of youth
the prime
of her life   with 2 sons
and a daughter
  one well   one epileptic
the daughter   married
at so young an age   her eyes
lowered
    into the valley

she sat in the rain
drinking in her fate
  her alcoholic husband
raging
like the storm above

she escaped
in the middle of the night

driving in
       desperation: the sizzle
  of tires
in her ears   the fine mist
   the drizzle
      the wind and water
streaming on
   the windshield
running from the cascade
looking for the comfort
that rain affords

until she found peace
      with a gentle man
during
   the showers of light
and dark October

suburban split
level   with friends
and family
     lobster gleaming
at new year's   trips to
Japan   dance recitals and daycare centres
hearty companion laughter
     long into night
with
   clothes marinating
  in cigarette
smoke   for years
afterward.

for sons and grandsons:
[rising cadences of collapsing
weather cascade to
(the ground]
    is wet
with her memory)

her eyes are like circles
on the cusp between
illness and death as she
listens
    to the rhythm
over and over   of rain

Yeah, the road
through the Delta is smooth
sun-drenched   but with her
before me
    I could
see
    the
        premonition
of a swirling devil's wind
and cloudbursts on the horizon

the myth
    of rain
is that it ends.

like her.

U[ta-go]koro

Mango Summer

When the *kona* winds
flow
      from the south,
they howl
  like monsters
so loud with mouths
drooling
    in the ear;

mangoes
       plump
  on the trees
fall
    heavily
to the ground.

Sweetness
    seeps
through the skin
  and releases
into the air
thick   with humidity

bringing to mind
the sticky perfume
of childhood.

The Emperor of Stars

he sat in his stroller
on the slope
of a 2-car driveway

heaven curved above
as if bowing
       as if offering
the crown jewels
of moon and planets

his eyes widened
       his arms reached open
a star flared
and covered him
       with its dust

he smiled
and fell to dream

for Bunji

and I saw an angel
(beneath the Turner)

and I saw
       an angel
standing in the sun

stinging bodies riddled
with holes
       rivers of matter
and blood flowed
within the confines
of the picture
frame   ships splintered
before the winds of torment
the breath of God
antiquity
       arched
the sun
flashed blindly

    the angel calls
for the feast of vultures
as kings, captains,
mighty men,
horses and riders,
the free and enslaved,
small and great,
fall into the crimson
lake, bursting yellow
the paint of brimstone

and I saw
        the beast and
the kings of the earth
thrown into that lake
that burns
        like a nova

as my emperor son slept
beneath
        head bowed

mouth gurgling

National Gallery, London
Poem excerpt from "Voyage of Columbus"
by Samuel Rogers, 1810

and in my half-sleep/I heard Otōsan *leaving*

dark
    was still
with us
    just
  beginning
its struggle to hold
its empire

the door opened
with a yawn
to the cavern of outside

I whispered a goodbye
he half-intoned the same

I hope he heard me
wrapped in the emerging
blankets of morning.

Kiss of a Father

to know
        To Know
absolutely
sinew
        vessel
 synapse
hair   memory
        bone
completely
to breathe the blood
to taste the crying
to crack the marrow
        unequivocally

~~~

for a son
   to kiss his father
(not since
I was   a boy)
his shrivelled skin
recoiled   then relaxed

he smirked at the sentiment
before he sank deeper
into his dis-
ease

        he had begun to open
toward me
  but spoke no words.

(for a father
    to kiss his   [the
baby son) gurgles and laughs
        pliant skin
moving toward the callous
in the cold air
and light]

~~~

the fate of a son
is never
to know his father

A Simple Face

As I grow old
I look
      into the mirror
among the liquid images
to find my father's face
surfacing
from   the silver depths.

it has a simplicity
[
moulded by a lumber
camp   survivor of the
internment   scarred by
a construction site
and instilled with father
-hood]

a simplicity fixed in love
his face
        in mine

Talk Story

David's father
sat at the table,
his celestial face
that white men branded on him
settled into
a convivial demeanour

    laughter into night

he gave the advice
of friendship
as he *talk story* of catching fish
— when cooking fish
the skin must sizzle
soaking in the garlic and onions.

We sat
on comfortable couches,
he full with the pride
of a father,
his son about to begin
the wedding dance

    drinking into night

we ate the *shiu mai*
small dumplings of friendship
as he *talk story* of his own father
imprisoned
then murdered at the hands

of communists
for the ability to teach.

      fading in the night

he lies
in a hospital bed
unaware of his wasting body

he *talk story* no more
but those he saved
from Tiananmen
stand in gratitude   (around him)

they softly pray

david,
we have heard the stories
fathers tell sons
        it is now time to join hands

and *talk story*
to our sons.

for dr. edward wong

Childhood

the light
       from the hallway
creeps   in-
to the bedroom
  dust seeking coherence

like smoke in
still air
       words
   float up -ward
to the 2nd floor ceiling

    only to drift down
the walls
       to tickle like mere whispers
in a dream
  conversations not in a
hurry to dis-
appear

words & light
       like a slow
tumble of thunder
as my eyes
           liquefy
and then close
  shut with
the glue of night
in
      a fall
to sleep.

Counting Kōden

Blackie Ohara, $50.00; Hammerhead Toyota, $100.00; Mr. and Mrs. Nagatomi in sympathy, $25.00; Chips and Chop Tanaka, $50.00; Aunt Vicky, $100.00; Sumi Ohashi, $25.00; Blue Matsueda, $10.00 . . .

    Counting *kōden*
    by the kitchen light.

    a degree of memory
    in the amount
        a gesture of respect
    with every dollar
    a measured
    sum that is always exact
       that is equal to what was given
    when *kōden*
    was counted last

    it is hot
        humid august air
    will not release its grip

    a sad trio
        counting *kōden,*
    into the middle
    of night:

    the widowed husband
    abandoned sister, orphaned daughter.

when the full moon
turns the water turquoise
and the stairs clearly
descend
       to the bottom
of the pool
where she lies in state

       arms crossed
       over her thin chest,
       the bones holding them up
       like the braces of a bridge

and the three-year-old
in bed cannot sleep   will not
       sleep
as the heat weighs heavily

(she died a quiet death —
       as a grandmother

with him by her bed
she touched
       his cheek with a wish . . .
and a kiss
a sweet goodbye)

counting *kōden*: Michiko and Hank Sugimoto,
$20.00; Frank Kawasaki, $100.00; Kay Shintani
with condolences, $10.00 . . .

they stop a moment
to hear a promising
rustle of wind outside

"grandma is making a little breeze for us . . . "
he calls
        from the bedroom
a small voice in the dark

Kona Weather

the air was still
    as if trapped
inside a coffin
    the pooling heat
stuffy, like wet cotton

flies hung suspended
the palms bent
    backs stiff and creaking
(accustomed
to the prevailing wind)
at a loss in the stagnant air

the setting in of *kona* weather

sound
carried across the sweating skies

the sound of traffic
  thick with
ozone
    the sound of tempers
breaking   the sound
of a six-year-old
screaming at the moment
her father died.

    kona weather
strips away
the mask the trades
bring
    to paradise.

for jeff song

Broken Moon

A broken moon,
its water
        poured
through the colander clouds
as light
upon
        the neighbourhood.

A broken moon
    rose the night
she visited one last time.

        don't call her ghost
        or phantom
                or devil

        call her okāsan
        who stroked my back,
                tickled her child,
        to let me know
        all was well,

        she was home

Her face rose
as a broken moon
        until the clouds
folded in & over
leaving me
        to the depths
of my own sleep.

Sisters

my sister
    never liked me
but that was all right
what could i do?
her bad luck was my fault
so she said   as the middle one

she hobbles
down
dark hallways
secure knowing
the chair waits
for her to sit
and read
the nightly paper.

    my youngest sister
left for adventure
and fortune   she
married a good man
and never returned

the evening shades
draw slowly to close
it's time for bed.

    they thought
i was the good one
who stayed at home
to care for mother
but i wonder

at the ache of my arms
never squeezed
    at the burn of lips
never pressed

legs
    crackle
like   kindling
  window drapes
flutter
   and snap
as ghosts howl
on trade winds.

he could have been
a drunk
        [alcoholic fists to a sister's face
he could have been
the father
       of my children
      the wailing harmony of babies]
why must I be the good one?

garbled sentences
punctuated by the occasional scream
in her sleep
       every night
as she converses
with sister ghosts
gone mad

The Swimming Pool

    the still
            bluemarine
    of water
        beneath
     a riverflow sky

    the surface
          does ripple
    from time to time
    as the trades
    pull alcohol-wet
    cool sheets
    across the islands
     evaporating
         light
    fractures into diamonds
              at the bottom
        of the pool

    sprinklers sizzle
    over even, manicured lawns

    she sits
    her legs knitted to the wheelchair
       her hands
    fossils on her lap

           I used to swim every day
           in this pool, you know —
           for twenty years
                    good health

> *strong legs*
> *strong . . .*

    mucus and tears
    the voice falters

drawn toward the water
  the feel of it rushing by
the spray blown into air

Tie waterwings
to the wheels
      Float across the surface
Release the air
and Sink
      into the familiar
wet and current.

but she sits
and wonders:

    are the plumeria in bloom?

Nightclouds

a flock of
 wildboys
swarming up a hill
towards home
heralds
the approach of night-
fall
   the dark
       intruder creeps
across building faces
one by one   curtain
       eyes close
and beasts wail
to the beat of trashcans
   while newspapers
dance in the isolating wind

and in the
       deeper
dark of bed sheets
an ocean
swells and collapses

with the need for breath

as whitecaps of skin
glow in gathering
moon-
   light

the upper winds
begin
to rip apart
the nightclouds

Eating Figs with Mrs. Long

in a room
of chinese modern
water
        dripped into
  porcelain —
the echo of hearts
        engaged in in-
consequential conversation

I ate figs
with Mrs. Long

the purple flesh
collapsed in-
ward red juice
coated the lips
seeds lodged
between teeth

I asked af-
ter her daughters
  she told me
of her generous mother
who gave
     American silver dollars
to the poor —

(a shower of coins
glittering in the sun
wetting the smiles)

I spoke of
her husband
  she bragged
of a banquet
in the Great Hall
      and of Chou En lai
who smiled upon her
— like a god

I in-quired
about
    her health
she whispered,
"money
     is power"

~~~

purple flesh
collapses juices co-
mingle
  sweat beads on skin
cold numb lips

eating figs with
Mrs. Long
     iced fruit
on wet porcelain
during a humid afternoon

Lushlife

Romance is mush
Stifling those who would strive.
I'll live a lush life
in some small dive.
And there I'll be
While I rot with the rest
Of those whose lives are lonely too.
      — *Billy Strayhorn*

a sea of air
 anchored by steel columns
sunk
   in its depths
lies within the hull of an
abandoned factory,
a titanic
decaying in rust
and silence

[without drama or tragedy]

he sits
behind a clapboard
wall of anonymous companies
amongst paint cans, order
forms and rejected design,
breathing
in the lead exhaling
the bar smoke
of long ago small dives.

he sits
before the up-
right piano   its ribs exposed
the soundboard cracked
   cigarette traces
the burn
   of ruined women
along the run of wood
around the fake-
ivory keys

                 through
wired windows,
smeared with the grime
of commerce,
he ponders   slate skies
and the elegance of
a bill evans diminished

he sets fingers
to broken teeth,
      their tips grown black
and crusted with
limited life, and begins to play.

the strains of billy stray-
horn
      coltrane's blues
(still) in some dive
modalities of the chord progression
      augmentation
syncopation

      clusters of notes
in the staccato movement
of
    jagged jazz

i met her back in '62
in one of those coffee bars
on avenue rd.

angular women
all legs
and mascara
  smoke dancing above
the thelonious
    "After Midnight"
playing perpetually

another one was a musician,
classically trained,
she intimidated me   she suggested
the goatee
    one of those trips hip cats were digging

she left me to go have a baby.

closeted talk.
the rapture
of the dark over-
comes.
the scene is *serene*
turns *mean* in the bebop
of noise twisted over

flattened
> out
> smoothed out

and turned into the "typing" of the beat
and the "chinese music" of the bop

i dream of my lost sister
from time to time
> *we were so poor*

after my mother died i
practised
on a cardboard keyboard
> *she died too*

taking care of us —
of t.b.

art
> poverty

and consumption
sisters
> of grace, the artist's muse

ambient light
> swells

within the room
of spilled paint and
broken improvisation
emanating   through-
out
> through the dull air

echo
> half-notes

become whole, heavy

and fall
        like a softrain
on parched floorboards

groundcover rapidly
spreads
            young shoots
on branches push
to the surface rush and flare
open to redefine the fact-
ory space
            spreading
      leaves
into the fullness of growth —

the thick of
vegetation
        dark nude women
with gleaming eyes
(partially concealed . . .)
stay in the shadows
           crying beasts
prowl beneath
the heavy green

a preponderance of Rousseau

yet he continues to play
living out the jungles
of his lushlife

for Roy Miya

a light rain in New Orleans

the rainfall
      of light fragments
in New Orleans
cleans the street

New Orleans: walled in
by the wrought-iron
victorian
      grace that
once were the houses
of blue light
    the music
cleans
   the street
of stale perfume
liquor and monoxide
      swirls
down
     sewer mouths

yet the neon
of cocktail take-out
and bottomless
women and cups
of hurricane   buzz
through till dawn

and the music,
ah, the music upon heaven's wings
of an old satchmo
     and ladyday

diminished
by the blues and
revered by withered drunks
who break off
shards of glass   in tribute

the ground grows wet with
piss
        and blood.
the fragment rain
        showers
the street
as fat cops question
a man
who shot his daughter
with a gun
        that went off in a riff
of jagged jazz during a
Night in Tunisia

[on the late night news
from fabled
bourbon street.

sirens scream,

Beneath the Southern Cross

the city
      with ambitions
to be new york
is too polite
all smiles]
      not enough crime
   too mindful
of its own colour
to be the new jerusalem

the cambodianbrazilburmese
the arabicmiddle easternvietnamese
spill
    from
 the airport
      at Botany Bay
criminals and holy men still

the scented herbs of
cigarette smoke mixes
with the swarm
of languages at intersections
of red lights

the cameroon
taximen
      the smooth asian
waiters
  the indonesian hucksters
the nepalese
      counter girls

hongkong town
   alleys
spread their clutter

everyone on the make
everyone on the take
talk the walk
     walk the talk

cell phones beeping in a chorus
  of need & desire
to live in the suburbs
     with the japanese
retired in their   smiling
 pink   houses
on manicured lawns

still
the Southern Cross
shines overhead
     pointing the way
to jerusalem. perhaps

Sidney, Australia

By the Buddha Bar

down by
        Grant
and Washington

where young chinese girls
run the streets

        pale chinese girls
with bare legs
long hair
    with sharp-angled
expressions on
their faces   run
the back lanes
in the shadows
of parental guidance
        a flowered sweater
short skirt   slippers
flip-flop

down by
    the corner
of presidents

where the sax player
blows out a string
of wayne shorter
in the archway of the Leung Fung
restaurant
        a traffic jam of
conversational chatter

to riff off —
      lonesome jazz
in a pedestrian flow
where tourists listen
and waiters and bus-
boys buzz to the music

down by
      the Buddha Bar

inside shadows
smile alcohol
    memories
smile talking
about Frankie Chan or Eddie
Chin before
    they took on
their american coats
and forgot their names

bent over the bar,
their bodies collapsed,
their hair pasted to the head,
they pull in the *karma*
from the running girls.

they raise their glasses
to the assumed beat
of some white guy
playing sax outside.

San Francisco, California

Seattle: pacific jazz

jazz, an inspired
    jazz,
an asian kind of jazz
flows from the fingertips
— the bass intertwines
      a flashpoint trumpet
keeps time in the shadows,

the sip of chartreuse

on a hot august night
   i sit   steam
drifting [as it were]
      the *kimono*
alight atop
the deep *taiko* rhythms
the grace of their hands; the passion
of fingertips

a ruby smile
from across the room
submerges
    beneath
the pacific jazz

10,000 Views of Diamond Head

a great wave
of light   erupts
above honolulu
      from *ewa* to
diamond head

fireworks
above lavaflow
kick up,
    explode in an arc
and fall into
the churning city

rapid-fire
      packs of 10,000
firecrackers
— the war cries
of the *coup d'etat*

the old year succumbs

a vision of Hokusai

oshōgatsu
    is the wave
that tosses
    the *tai*
into its curve of luck
    that promises fertility

with the *kazunoko*
in the seaspray and spume

that ripens the *mikan*,
shapes the *mochi*,
in the offertory to ancestors

a vision of diamond head
rises above the smoke
and thin red paper
 as demons burn away

in the wake of the new year

Paper Lanterns in August

A mosquito sting
    lets you know you're alive.

paper lanterns
down the Ala Wai canal
   to the sea
surrounding Honolulu:

it is Obon:
  the living wait
in the dark
    for the lantern
boats
  bearing ancestor names
to float past

~~~

chōchin,
    as diaphanous as
a man-of-war
fat
   like a luminous
puffer fish,
swayed in the satin breeze
   at the approach
of Obon

excited reflections
of a moon
    above water

conjured up
the lost, the long dead,
out of humidity and shadows

for their summer-long visit

$\sim\sim\sim$

the chanting hums
      the dancers circle
the incense hangs like
ghosts over
      water
and the *fue* mourns
in a minor key

goodbye
    goodbye
to yellow ghosts

trade winds howl
through the palms and
pull on conversations
      until there is nothing
but the still night
and the persistent buzz
of mosquitoes

      at the heart
of each lantern is a candle,

its light
>	yellow and anxious for wax and air
black water swirls,
>	slaps against each boat
until paper walls are soaked
and lanterns collapse in on themselves

>	only a hint of smoke escapes
>	the spirits flutter in their farewell

If the mosquito sting
>	is a reminder of life,

then the paper lantern is the fate to come.

City of Fallen Angels
(excerpts from *Paradise Lost*)

The waves of Malibu:
the serenity in the continuous
breaking of whitecaps.

Mist moves in from off shore
to wet the green   sloping
hills. Waves move
onto sand   pulling   in
rocks and pebbles
in their drag back to the sea.
Seagulls move over head
caught still in the motion
of wind and tide.

The breakers stand fixed before the fall.

On the streets of LA
where the Rebel Angels arise

> *impious War in Heav'n and Battle proud*
> *With vain attempt.*

They rage and collapse with hideous ruin and
combustion
down to bottomless perdition, there to dwell
in penal fire.

A simple man, with distorted face
and darting eyes,
    Rodney King,
almost trembling, cannot master
the words that will silence
the mad cries,
the beasts of hunger
the twin wolves of greed and murder.

> *Round he throws his baleful eyes*
> *that witness'd huge affliction and dismay*
> *mixt with obdurate pride and steadfast hate.*

And the vulgar media
switches on its dispassionate eye.

> The City of Angels is a city in
> flames. After two days of rioting,
> looting and killing, Los Angeles
> looks like a war zone. And there are
> fears that the flames will spread to
> engulf the entire United States in race
> riots.

Fires of no light
serve only to discover sights of woe,
regions of sorrow,
doleful shades
where peace and rest can never dwell,
hope never comes.

Unconsumed sulphur of the mind
is ever-burning
        far removed from the light
and waves of Malibu.

The seat of desolation:
lonely yellow eyes
set against the black sea of skin
look to God
and question His dark designs.

The grain of video
runs like a river at night.
Arms of thunder rise and collide
with the victim
for whom no point of light shines.
Jackboots of endless pain
kick to the small of the back
and his hand reaches for mercy
above the river of video
in the middle of the city.

Who can watch and not be moved?

Void of light,
Save what the glimmering of these livid flames
Casts pale and dreadful.

> the grey of black and white
> the ire of black and yellow

Latasha Harlins torn apart by naked fire
Soon Ja Du shakes in horror
the grey fades to black
        and a family defends its store
in koreatown
on a land with the stability of liquid fire.

And where is the lost Arch-Angel,
Martin Luther King,
now that the Stygian flood
has come again?

It is clear
No apostate angel may again utter the sweet
words:

> *Free at last! Free at last! I am free at last.*

High above the coast,
the wondrous constellation Orion,
bent and starry armed,
splits the sea to allow
escape from perfidious hatred,

The Abject and Lost lie down
in the sheer amazement of their change
and the once transfixed waves
come crashing down
in a drowning gulf.

But far within
And in thir own dimensions like themselves
The great Seraphic Kings and Cherubim
In close recess and secret conclave sat
A thousand Demi-Gods on golden seats,
Frequent and full. After short silence then
And summons read, the great consult began.

Another Home
1959 Japan

Blue whales wave goodbye
among Fukui whitecaps.

Winter clouds unfurl
    home again
potted flowers
in the
    sewing room

for matsujiro watada, 1906 – 1987
100 Mile Camp, B.C., 1942

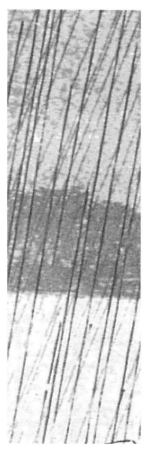

Nikkei Monogatari:
*Impressions of the Japanese-
Canadian Internment Experience*

A View from "The Orchard"

The moon travels
above a concentration camp
reflection
       in the eyes
a vision of freedom.

for seitaro takenaka, 1903 – 1994
New Denver, B.C., 1942 – 1943

The Irony of First Snow

The air is heavy,
fecund   like
a late pregnancy.

Distant peaks already
grow white
as salt shaker clouds
sprinkle snow
on barren rock.

The wind is tense
among the trees
that creak
   and mutter.

Frosted ground
feels crisp
beneath the feet
    as if to invite
the coming storm.

> *The Japanese of '42*
> *embraced the beauty*
> *of first snow*
> *even as they felt*
> *Sandon's valley close in*
> *smothering them*
> *in the grip of a clenched fist*
>
> *and the sun dragged across the mountain peaks*
> *pulling back the covers revealing the barren prison rock.*

Branches are heavy
with whiteness
as I wander
into
       the valley of the shadow.

for Kay Mizuno, 1920 –
Sandon, B.C., 1942 – 1945

Stillness

the October stillness
of a stand   of forest
in
    the
mountains
of hidden prisons
settles
in my heart

smoke from crude
shacks
      curls
into air   slowing
to stiffen into cold
columns
   of twisted fate

and undergrowth
full of bramble   thorns
and waste
        silent
discarded
branches   decaying leaves
   autumn's dead
their prone bodies flattened
      against the curve
of camp grounds
and government decrees

i can no longer hope
* . . . there's no hope . . . the baby*

is crying . . . the travel . . . constant
bumping on broken roads
into darkness   into
nothingness

listen   listen
    to the voices
crackling
in the cold-shocked air
voices filled with the wind

botchan, stop crying . . . we'll be there
soon . . . soon we'll be there

streams thicken   waterflow
  white over
rocks slows to a molasses
pace
    until it stops
altogether
as the voices continue

can't you stop . . . please stop . . .
stop . . .

the stillness overwhelms
and the dead crush
like summer insects under
foot

>   *that's good botchan . . .*
> *now sleep . . . sleep . . . stay quiet*
> *and all will be well . . . all will . . . be*
> *well . . .*

                  all comes to a standstill
until the smoke
    of cremation rises
before me and
above the lost landscape in sharp relief

a mother collapses into her own
dark paralysis

the october stillness
is disturbed
      by a gentle snowfall

tears have hardened and grown cold over the
years

> *for kinosaki,* infant, *1941 – 1942*
> *Sandon, B.C., 1942*

Wild Strawberries and Mushrooms

Wolves
call to each other
    about a fresh
kill
      beneath
the frostlight of a full moon.

          Their howls skid
across the crystal surface of snow and ice.
Shivers up the spine.

Secret fields of *matsutake*
are dormant
while *yama-neko* snarl at one another.

But the wild strawberries
are sweet
and bring back summer
with the simple
opening of a jar.

for hideno nomura, 1902 – 1998
Roseberry, B.C., winter 1942

Moon Above the Ruins

There is only the moon
      above
the ruins of Tashme.

Takeo came out
of his internment cabin
playing his *shakuhachi*

    his breath
    blowing dry through the bamboo
    tunnel of that instrument

minor notes bent to the wind
rose to the parched, mad moon
during that early august

one by one
the other prisoners
emerged
into the dry light
looking for the sun
that was never
to rise again
      we sought
the warmth of each other
   we knew that time
was over
      one by one
we left the camp
and ventured in-
to the cool mountain

breezes
that came down and blew
through our shrinking selves

arid cracked voices   drew
together and rode
bareback
on the hollow notes
of that old flute
until the rock mountain faces
      sang back to us
an ancient pentatonic
song

there is only the moon
since the august sun
exploded over hiroshima
      burning paper cranes
and freezing shadows
          during the cusp of sunrise
and moonset.

for hisashi goromaru
Hiroshima-ken, 1910 – 1987
Tashme, B.C., 1942 – 1945

The Sound of a Train

The sound
  of a train is true,
the way it rings
      in still air
as it curves
  around a rock
face.

Its wind pushes
against me
as it scrabbles
to get by,
its wheels like claws
against the ground.

And in the distance,
a smoke trail
reveals where it's been,
the long drawn out whistle
calling out to its destination.

When the mounties
told me I needed a permit
to meet the train at the station
even if it was just to say goodbye
to fellow Japanese,

I went to the bend in the river
and waved to them
as the sound of the train
fades into obscure
memory.

for tsunisuke okimoto, 1903 – 1987
Greenwood, B.C., 1942 – 1987

An Empty Field

in the clear
      bright air
of mountains and
forest

mist rises
    a green aura
dances
before the eyes

That's where
old lady Popoff lived. In the
house on the hill
  watching
over us.
      She rented
the field
to the government for its legal purposes.

the rows of shacks
      dragged dust
along roads
to imprison their inmates
      meagre tar paper shacks
never
meant to stand against snow and ice

the shouts of baseball boys
passing away time
to nightfall

                    while men
no longer able
to provide slumped
to the ground   in front of
hollow door-
ways

and still no one
     moved
even with the screams of
terror from
        a 4-year-
old
     drowning
in the nearby
river

Nice lady but
she made a lot o' money
on us.

the field
        is empty
only mist
    and wind
remain carrying with them
the muffled cries
of 1942

>   *for Reverend Kenryu Tsuji, 1920 –*
>   *Slocan, B.C., 1942 – 1944*

Bury Your Horses

Horses, horses, horses!
Catching sight of a cemetery
— *bury your horses!*
                the child
squealed in victory.

Grade one students
stood in a row
holding out a trembling hand
half whimpering, half
wondering.
    The teacher,
a *nisei*,
        walked down the line
and struck each offering
with the flat side of a ruler.

You won't speak Japanese any more!
Childish crying,
a vow never to speak again.

Kissing played
the Community Hall,
on a cranking projector,
captivating a six-year-old.
    The next day,
she reached across the aisle
and kissed Freddy Kakuno
on the cheek.
He jumped and screamed,
OW, get me out of here!

The one room school
remains mute in ruin.

Deer meat
felled by a single invisible
wire between trees:
   the carcass of twisted limbs,
soaking blood and dead eyes
       coyotes howled
with the smell of fresh kill.

The echo from peak
to rock face
       vibrated
in the trembling of hands,
    the night
of wild horses stampeding
down
the mountainside.
 Stay in your cabins!
From beneath
the table and chairs
        (the thunder of hooves
        and the bloodied eyes)
she began
the years of night-mare.

She stands among the tumbleweeds
and cactuses
    drying her lungs
with every breath.

In plain view of a cemetery
— *bury your horses* —
the woman
scatters her memories.

for Shirley Yamada, 1941 –
Midway, B.C., 1942 – 1949

A Funeral in the Mountains

he crashed through
  the surface
into
      water
and black ice

his eyes froze into cubes

the dead
      of winter
roared
  enraged
[the reciting of *Nembutsu*
during *otsuya*
         ]

he still roars
   with
the
     blizzard
  wind
[in their haunting of mountains]

a funeral pyre
     of iced cedar and
  sluggish smoke

for tsuyoshi asada, 1918 – 1942
Tashme, B.C., 1942

GLOSSARY

botchan — term of affection for a baby boy

chōchin — paper lantern

ewa — Hawaiian pidgin term for "toward the west side"

fue — small wooden flute

Fukui — province of Japan

hinomaru — the Japanese flag

Hokusai — Japanese woodblock print artist, (1760 – 1849)

kami — god(s)

kazunoko — herring roe

ko — a term of affection for a child, suffix for a woman's given name

kōden — a monetary offering to a departed spirit, a condolence gift

kona — Hawaiian pidgin term for humid weather

matsutake — a kind of wild mushroom

mikan — mandarin orange

mochi — pounded rice cake

monogatari — a story, a narrative

Nembutsu — an expression of gratitude to the Buddha (Namu Amida Butsu)

nikkei — Japanese North American

nisei — second-generation Japanese Canadian

Obon — Buddhist festival of light honouring ancestors

okāsan — mother

oshōgatsu — New Year's day

otsuya — a wake

otōsan — father

shakuhachi — bamboo flute

shiu mai — Chinese dumplings

tai — sea bream, a good-luck fish

taiko — Japanese drum

talk story — Hawaiian pidgin for "shooting the breeze"

utagokoro — poetry

yama-neko — mountain lion